194968

# HOW IT WAS

# THE ROMAN EMPIRE

*Dorothy Metcalf*

B. T. Batsford Ltd, London

# CONTENTS

First published 1995

Typeset by Goodfellow & Egan Ltd, Cambridge

and printed in Hong Kong

Published by
B. T. Batsford Ltd
4 Fitzhardinge Street
London W1H 0AH

A CIP catalogue record for this book is available from the British Library.

ISBN 0 7134 7435 1

**Cover illustration:** *Scenes of banqueting, Pompeii.*

**Frontispiece:** *A Pompeiian girl chews her pen in the search for just the right word.*

# INTRODUCTION

For 800 years from the third century BC (before the birth of Christ) to the fifth century AD (anno domini meaning in the year of our Lord) the city of Rome was at the centre of an empire around the Mediterranean sea, that at its height was 4,000 kilometres from west to east, and 3,700 kilometres from north to south.

We know a great deal about this Roman world of 2,000 years ago from three main sources. Firstly, many of its buildings, monuments and roads remain, and there are thousands of pieces of writing on stones, such as gravestones. Secondly, we have the writings of Roman historians, poets, politicians and generals, and thirdly, there is the work of archaeologists, uncovering the past on sites all over Europe.

In the course of its long history, Rome had several forms of government. From 510 BC it was a republic, ruled by two consuls elected annually, who were advised by the Senate, a kind of parliament composed of wealthy, influential nobles. In 81 BC a general called Sulla seized power, and Rome became a dictatorship. He died not long after and the power of the Senate was restored, but 30 years later Julius Caesar became dictator in his turn. He was murdered, and it was as a result of the civil war that followed that Caesar's great-nephew Octavian (known later as the first Emperor Augustus) became sole ruler.

You may be saying to yourself, 'But what's this to do with us?' It has a surprising amount to do with us. Britain was part of the Roman Empire for four hundred years. Many of our towns were begun by the Romans. A great number of our words come from Latin, the Roman language. We sometimes use Roman numerals (look at your television screen for the dates that programmes were made, for example). Many of our roads follow the line of roads constructed by Roman soldiers. Some of our laws are copied from Roman laws. It was the Romans who first had central heating, public baths, a fire brigade, and a postal service (a kind of Pony Express for official letters).

Yet, if a time machine were to take us back to the Roman Empire most of us would find life very different and very difficult. We would work hard for long hours for low wages, food would be plain, and there probably wouldn't be a great deal of it, and ordinary homes would be very uncomfortable indeed. For women, especially, life was very restricted. We know that many must have worked outside their homes – we have the tombstones of a fishmonger, a dressmaker and a hairdresser, but it would have been unthinkable to have worked at many of the jobs we consider it normal for women to do today. And however rich their families, they had few legal rights, and could not vote.

We shall see how Roman government brought greater prosperity to some people in the provinces of the Empire. But might they not have preferred the freedom to decide their own fate to a foreign governor backed by an army of occupation? Here is the view of a philosopher called Epictetus, who lived in Rome, but who was expelled in 89 AD by the Emperor Diocletian.

**In Rome, reckless men are trapped by soldiers. A soldier in civilian clothing sits down beside you and begins to vilify (criticise) the emperor. Just because he began the abuse, you too, say what's on your mind – and the next moment you are handcuffed and led away.**

## Introductory quiz

### Do you know?

What is the origin of the saying 'All roads lead to Rome'?

How a Roman soldier was punished for falling asleep on duty?

Who grew cabbages in his retirement?

What a Roman meant if he said, 'You could play micatio with him in the dark'?

Who took a team of elephants over the Alps?

What is the name of the Roman Emperor who was given his name because of the kind of shoes he wore?

# BEGINNINGS OF EMPIRE

By the second century AD the Roman Empire stretched from the edge of the Sahara desert in Africa northwards to Britain, and from Spain in the west to the mountains of Turkey and what is now Israel and Syria in the east. The Romans were the only people ever to unite this immense area around the Mediterranean sea.

There is a legend that Rome was founded beside the river Tiber in 753 BC by Romulus, who with his twin brother Remus, was brought up by a wolf. What we know for sure is that 250 years later Rome was a thriving republic, that is, a country without a king or a queen. It was ruled instead by two consuls, each elected for one year, who were advised by the Senate, a group of rich ex-magistrates. The magistrates in their turn were elected by the Assembly, which consisted of all Roman citizens. Women and slaves did not have a vote. By the middle of the third century BC Rome was the most important city in Italy, having driven back invading tribes from the north, and having conquered colonies of Greeks in the south.

Rome's first foreign province was the island of Sicily, which was captured in 241 BC. Another large city, Carthage, had grown up on the coast of North Africa, not far from present day Tunis. Carthage and Rome became rivals over both trade and industry, and there were three wars between them. In the first, Sicily was captured, in the second the Carthaginian leader Hannibal attacked Rome itself, but was defeated, and in the third Carthage was completely destroyed. The Romans subsequently built their own city on its ruins.

Rome had enemies in the east as well. Philip of Macedon had allied himself with Hannibal, and began to build up his own armies along the Aegean coast. Fortunately for Rome, other Greek states were afraid Macedonia would become too powerful, and they united to defeat Philip, allowing Rome to conquer all of Greece by 148 BC. In 133 BC the province of Asia was established, and this included many Greek cities.

The next 100 years saw the Empire grow bigger still, and after many wars Gaul (present-day France), Spain, Cyprus and much of North Africa came under Roman control. In Italy and Rome itself, however, the first century BC was a time of great unrest. The wars had made many farmers poor, some politicians were concerned more with making themselves rich than the good of the state, and armies sometimes gave their loyalty to their generals rather than to the Senate. This unrest led to many years of civil war, that is one group of people within a country fighting against another.

In 49 BC Julius Caesar, the general in charge of the army in Gaul, crossed the river Rubicon, the river that was the boundary between Gaul and Italy, at the head of his army. Roman law expressly forbade that a general should cross the Rubicon with his troops, and in so doing Caesar made clear his intention of seizing power for himself. He defeated his former friend Pompey, the champion of the Senate, and in 44 BC was declared dictator. His victory, however, was short-lived. In the same year he was stabbed to death on the steps of the Senate by a group of nobles, led by Brutus and Cassius. Caesar's friend Mark Antony and his great-nephew Octavian killed Brutus in the further wave of civil war that followed, and ruled the republic between

(Below left) *The temple of Concorde, Agrigento, Sicily. Sicily was Rome's first foreign province.*

*Animals from one of Rome's African provinces being loaded on to a ship – possibly for use in a show in an amphitheatre.*

them, but they too quarrelled, and in 31 BC Octavian's navy destroyed Antony's forces at the sea-battle of Actium. Octavian, as Augustus, became Rome's first Emperor.

Under Augustus the empire continued to grow. In the first century AD Britain was subdued, and at the beginning of the second century AD the Emperor Trajan annexed land north of the river Danube, Armenia and part of Arabia. We know a great deal about Trajan's campaigns, largely because when he returned to Rome he built a column, and had carved on it pictures of his armies and their battles.

Today we disapprove of countries seizing other people's land by force, so why did the Romans pursue this policy? Sometimes they had to defend themselves, as against Carthage. They also liked booty – Strabo tells us that the Romans came to Britain for corn, cattle, gold, silver, iron, hides, slaves and hunting dogs – and they exacted heavy taxation from the provinces. But above all, they admired military glory, and qualities such as bravery and endurance. They felt they had the right to rule because their government was better, and they thought they could bring stability and order to barbarian peoples.

## Hannibal crossing the Alps

How Hannibal crossed the Alps into Italy on foot in winter in 218 BC is recounted here by Polybius, a Greek historian, writing in the second century BC.

> Next day he [Hannibal] broke up his camp and began the descent. During this he encountered no enemy, except a few skulking marauders [attackers], but owing to the difficulties of the ground and the snow his losses were nearly as heavy as on the ascent. The descending path was very narrow and steep, and as both men and beasts could not tell on what they were treading owing to the snow, all that stepped wide of the path or stumbled were dashed down the precipice . . . They at length reached a place where it was impossible for either the elephants or the pack animals to pass owing to the extreme narrowness of the path . . . and here the soldiers once more became disheartened and discouraged.
>
> (Polybius, *Histories III*).

Small wonder! Polybius goes on to tell us that Hannibal eventually got the animals down by building up the path. He also tells us that this crossing cost Hannibal fifty per cent of his men and animals.

*Model of a war elephant found at Carthage.*

**Q**

**What do you think are the advantages and disadvantages of using elephants on an expedition like this?**

*The Romans adopted the Greek idea of making their leaders gods. In this relief Julius Caesar (top centre left) is shown becoming a god.*

## Defeat in Gaul

Julius Caesar, the general in charge of the Roman army in Gaul, wrote his own account of his campaigns in *The Conquest of Gaul*. This is his account of a defeat at Gergovia in Southern Gaul in 52 BC.

> The next day Caesar paraded the troops, and reprimanded [scolded] them for their rashness and impetuosity. They had decided for themselves, he said, to advance further and attack the town, neither halting when the retreat was sounded, nor obeying the military tribunes and generals . . . 'Much as I admired the heroism you showed,' he went on, '. . . I cannot too strongly condemn your bad discipline and your presumption in thinking that you know better than your commander-in-chief'.
>
> **(Caesar, *The Conquest of Gaul*)**

In a passage a little before this, Caesar admits that 'the other legions did not hear the trumpet, because a fairly wide hollow intervened.'

## The Assassination of Julius Caesar

Cicero was a lawyer and politician of the first century BC, whose books, speeches and letters tell us a great deal about the politics of the day. Here he gives his opinion of Julius Caesar:

> Our tyrant deserved his death for having made an exception of the one thing that was the blackest crime of all . . . Behold, here you have a man who was ambitious to be king of the Roman people and master of the whole world; and he achieved it! The man, who maintains that such an ambition is morally right is a madman, for he justifies the destruction of law and liberty and thinks their hideous and detestable suppression glorious . . .
>
> **(Cicero, *On Duties*)**

Cicero was himself murdered by Caesar's ally Mark Antony.

In blaming his men for the defeat, in what light is Caesar trying to show his own actions? What might be his motive in doing so?

## CAN YOU REMEMBER ?

*Where was Carthage? Why were Carthage and Rome rivals?*
*Who made the first attempt to conquer Britain, and which Emperor in the end succeeded?*
*Why did the Romans want to rule a great empire?*

## THINGS TO DO

1  Try to visit your local museum to see what has been found of the Roman occupation of your area.
2  Imagine you are the governor of a new Roman province. Write a speech telling the inhabitants about the benefits of Roman rule (you might like to refer to the chapters on Life Under Roman Rule).
3  Here are some Latin words with their English meanings: unus – one, dominus – master, frigidus – cold, manus – hand, sedeo – I sit, video – I see. Can you think of any English words from these Latin ones?

In this passage Cicero uses words and phrases that suggest that his judgement of Caesar may not have been a balanced one. What are they? Do you agree that what Caesar did in taking power was 'the blackest crime of all'?

## CHECK YOUR UNDERSTANDING

Can you remember the meaning of the following?

booty            republic
legend           triumph

# THE EMPEROR AUGUSTUS

Julius Caesar was murdered in 44 BC in the Senate House and civil war followed. He had nominated as his successor his great-nephew Octavian, who was nineteen and studying in Greece. Octavian immediately returned to Rome, but it was not until 31 BC when he defeated his former ally Mark Antony (who subsequently committed suicide with Cleopatra of Egypt) that he took control of the Empire. He became known as Augustus Caesar, Augustus 'the dignified one' the name given him by the Senate, and Caesar, his adopted family name. He ruled for forty-five years, gave the Empire peace and prosperity, and was perhaps the greatest of the emperors of Rome.

Augustus had great personal authority over the Roman people, but from the beginning he said that he wished to rule according to law. He wrote that three times, 'the senate and people of Rome agreed that I should be appointed supervisor of laws and morals without a colleague and with supreme power, but I would not accept'. Nevertheless he did hold very real power. In 27 BC he was given the command for ten years of a province which included Spain, Gaul, Syria and Cilicia (see map on page 45), an area where twenty-two out of the twenty-five legions of the army were stationed. He was also *consul* until 23 BC (that is, one of the two magistrates who held the highest power in Rome), when he was made a *tribune* for life, which meant he could stop any law the Senate wished to make. In 2 BC he received the title *Pater Patriae*, Father of the Fatherland.

Augustus' power was based on the loyalty to himself and the Empire of three very powerful bodies: the army, the Senate and the middle classes. He reformed the army, recruiting *auxiliaries* (those who were not yet Roman citizens) and giving discharged soldiers land or money. More territory was annexed under Augustus than under any other leader in Rome's history. He changed the Senate

*The Roman theatre in Merida, Spain, built on the orders of Emperor Agrippa in 24 BC.*

into being more a group of administrators than a law-making assembly. He encouraged the *equites*, the middle-classes who up to this time had been excluded from public life, by appointing them to such posts as Prefect of the Praetorian Guard (the imperial bodyguard) and Prefect of the corn supply. All this gave the Empire strong and efficient government.

Many poets and writers were at work during Augustus' reign, for example, Virgil, who wrote the *Aeneid* – the story of the founding of Rome by Aeneas – and Livy, who wrote a history of Rome. Fine new buildings were erected, and artists and sculptors were encouraged. Augustus himself took over the administration of the city. The streets were policed by 'urban cohorts', commanded by the Prefect of the City. A conservancy board was set up, the 'curators of the river bank', to prevent the flooding of the Tiber, which over the years had drowned many people and undermined the foundations of buildings. Free distribution of corn was made to those in need, and from time to time gifts of money. There were many gladiatorial contests and public games for entertainment, and religious festivals were revived.

Despite these reforms, however, life for the majority of Rome's inhabitants was extremely hard, with barely enough to eat, and homes, that with only basic heating, light and sanitation, to us would seem uninhabitable.

Augustus himself never lived a life of luxury. In character he was cold and forbidding. There were many sadnesses in his family life, and one of his greatest disappointments was that he had no son left alive to succeed him. To a grandson (who died before he did) he wrote on his birthday, 'Greetings, dear Gaius, my most delightful little donkey, whom I always miss.'

## Britain at the Time of Augustus

Although more territory came under the control of Rome during the reign of Augustus than under any other Emperor, he made no attempt to conquer Britain.

> Though they could have held Britain, the Romans have not thought it worthwhile: there is nothing to fear from the Britons, for they are not strong enough to launch an attack across the channel, and there is little advantage in holding it, for it seems that at the moment we get more income from the customs duty, than the tribute could bring in, if you deduct the cost of maintaining an army to guard the island and collect the tribute.
>
> (Strabo, 2.5.8 (book published in Rome in 7 BC))

Customs duty would be collected by the Romans on British goods exported to Europe. The *tribute* was a tax levied on a conquered people. Strabo (who was a geographer) goes on to say that:

> Some of the chiefs there have won Augustus' friendship by sending ambassadors and paying court to him: they have made offerings on the Capitol.

**Q**

How would you sum up, firstly, the Romans' attitude to Britain at this stage, and secondly, the Britons' attitude to Rome?

## A Petition for Freedom

This is Augustus' answer to a petition for their freedom from the people of the island of Samos. It is inscribed on the wall of the theatre at Aphrodisias in Greece.

> You yourselves can see that I have given the privilege of freedom to no people except to the people of the Aphrodisians, who in the war took my side and were made captives, because of their goodwill towards us. For it is not right to bestow the greatest privilege of all without purpose and without cause. I am of goodwill towards you, and would be willing to favour my wife, who is zealous on your behalf, but not to the point of breaking my custom. For it is not the money I care about, which you pay into our tax system, but I am not willing to have the most valued privileges given to anyone without a reasonable cause.

The wife mentioned here is Livia, who was married to Augustus for fifty-three years. (She was, in fact, his third wife.)

*The Emperor Augustus founded the Praetorian Guard as an imperial body-guard.*

## CAN YOU REMEMBER ?

*Who was Augustus' chief rival for power, and how did he die?*
*What did the title 'Pater Patriae' mean?*
*Why was it important for Augustus to be consul in Spain, Gaul, Syria, and Cilicia?*
*In what ways did Augustus look after the ordinary people of Rome?*

## CHECK YOUR UNDERSTANDING

Can you remember the meaning of the following words?

equites
Praetorian Guard
tribute

## THINGS TO DO

1 One of the ways in which the Roman 'curators of the river bank' tried to prevent flooding was to build canals from the Tiber to draw off the water. You will know that flooding is still a major problem in many countries today. How have methods of flood control changed? Try to arrange a visit to the Thames Barrier or find a photograph of it to see one modern solution.
2 The *Aeneid* is the story of Aeneas, who, according to Virgil, founded Rome. Your local or school library will have a book about him. Write one of his adventures in your own words.

## The Res Gestae (Achievements)

Augustus asked that after his death, his account of his deeds and accomplishments, the *Res Gestae*, should be engraved on bronze tablets, and displayed in front of his burial tomb. The bronze tablets themselves have disappeared, but fragments of the text have been discovered. This extract was part of a text engraved on an inside wall of a temple at Ancyra (present-day Ankara in Turkey).

> Wars on land and sea both domestic and foreign throughout the whole world I often waged and as victor I spared all citizens who sought forgiveness. Foreign nations, who could be safely pardoned, I preferred to save rather than to cut down. Around five hundred thousand Roman citizens were under my military oath. Of these I sent out to colonies or sent back to their own towns ... somewhat more than three hundred thousand, and to all of these I assigned lands or gave them money as rewards for military service. I captured six hundred ships apart from those which were smaller than triremes.
>
> (Augustus, *Res Gestae*)

A trireme was a boat that could be rowed by three banks of oarsmen, one above the other.

Julius Caesar also wrote about his campaigns. Do you think we can entirely trust a person's own account of what he has achieved? Give reasons for your answer.

*Augustus in military dress.*

# LIFE UNDER ROMAN RULE

Many countries in the twentieth century have been invaded and occupied by an enemy army, and it is very often a very unpleasant experience. The government and administration of an Empire as big as the Roman Empire saw many changes in the course of its long history. Some of the provinces were under the direct control of the Emperor, the others were under the Senate, but almost everywhere the Romans created a military dictatorship, which took away the right of provincial people to rule themselves in matters of defence, the law and taxation.

Governors, appointed for not less than three years at a time, were sent out from Rome and were very powerful indeed. They were in charge of the legions stationed in their area, and they were also the chief law officers. Their main duty was to maintain law and order throughout the province. They were helped by a *ius iuridicus*, who was in charge of minor legal affairs (he could not impose the death penalty as a governor could) and by a *procurator*, who was responsible for collecting taxes.

Larger settlements had some degree of self-government. They had councils, whose chief officers, the magistrates, were in charge of local affairs such as the upkeep of roads and buildings, and the supply of water. The Emperor Augustus established provincial councils of which we know little except that their chief power was they could communicate directly with the emperor over the governor's head.

How this system was used or abused depended very much on individual character. The Emperor Caligula (37–41 AD), so called after the small soldier's boots (*caligae*) he wore as a child, was cruel and corrupt. The Emperor Claudius (41–54 AD) on the other hand invited citizens from the provinces to become members of the Senate in Rome. Besides the curtailment of their freedom, one of the chief complaints of the provinces against Rome was the level of taxation. There were taxes on land, on individual wealth and goods, and there were death duties and customs duties. Cassius Dio, writing at the beginning of the third century, said of the Emperor Caracalla (211–217AD), 'he took pains to strip, despoil and grind down all the rest of mankind'.

What of the benefits of Roman rule? One of the greatest was the encouragement of the growth of towns. Many old tribal centres such as St Albans greatly increased in size, and Augustus himself founded more than seventy new cities. Some

(Above right) *Tax collector collecting money.*

*The city of Glanum in France.*

towns, Gloucester among them, were built especially for veteran soldiers, who when they had finished their service wished to remain in the country in which they had served. These new Roman towns had a central *forum*, a large open space where markets often took place and which was surrounded by fine buildings used as offices and lawcourts. There were also temples and shops. Some towns had an amphitheatre (a large, circular or oval open space, with seats rising in tiers around for spectacles of different kinds), and public baths.

Another benefit was the building of thousands of miles of roads all over the Empire. These roads were built in the first place so that the legions could move relatively quickly from place to place, but they were used by a great variety of people. Farmers could take their produce to market, there was a postal system for official letters, people from the provinces were able to travel to Rome either to see the sights or to take their petitions to the Emperor, and officials could more quickly go about their business.

Greater ease of communication also meant the spread of the Roman way of life. Many people living in Rome and Italy saw in the Empire an opportunity to make a better life for themselves abroad, and as well as those who became merchants and traders, many families settled permanently in Spain, the Rhineland, Africa and Asia Minor, taking with them the Latin language, and Roman dress and social customs.

Roman citizenship was much prized throughout the Empire. A citizen was protected by law from harsh treatment and certain punishments. He could vote in elections, and he had the right to have a legal case heard in Rome by the Emperor himself, as St Paul did. In the first two centuries AD citizenship was extended to more and more people by successive emperors. It could be granted to individuals, perhaps to auxiliaries as a reward for military service, or it might be given to whole communities. In 212 AD, finally, all free members of the Empire were made citizens.

A greater degree of prosperity was the result of Roman rule for certain classes of people within the Empire, chiefly farmers and merchants. Some wealthy provincial families grew to enjoy luxuries introduced by the Romans, and built for themselves large comfortable country villas and town houses in the Roman style, with central heating, bathrooms and beautiful mosaic floors. But for the vast majority of people in the provinces, their lives went on not so very differently after the Roman conquest as before. Their chief preoccupations continued to be getting enough to eat, and keeping warm. Now, with the Romans, they had to pay their taxes as well.

## Corrupt Government

Some governors were very good ones, and did not try to make themselves rich. Some, however, were not so – of the people named in this extract, Lollia Paulina became the Emperor Caligula's third wife and Marcus Lollius was the first governor of Galatia. (You will find an explanation of Roman money on page 46).

> I have seen Lollia Paulina covered in emeralds and pearls interlaced with each other and shining all over her head, hair, ears, neck and fingers, their total value amounting to 40,000,000 sesterces . . . they were not presents from an extravagant emperor but heirlooms acquired actually with the spoils of the provinces. This is the outcome of plunder, it was for this that Marcus Lollius disgraced himself by taking gifts from kings throughout the East . . . that his granddaughter might glitter in the lamplight covered with 40,000,000 sesterces.
>
> (Pliny, *Natural History* IX)

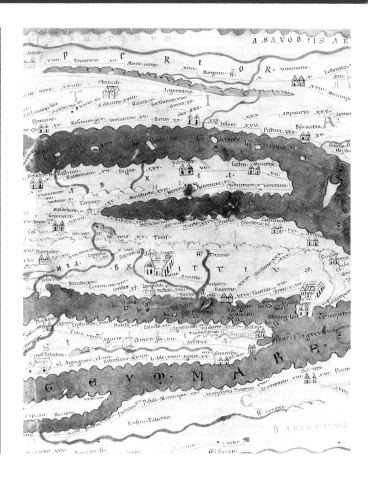

*The Peutinger map, a medieval copy of a late Roman map of the Empire shows southern Italy, Sicily and North Africa.*

Should people in powerful positions receive high salaries? Marcus Lollius did not. Give reasons for your answer.

## THINGS TO DO

1  Who is in charge of local government where you live? What are their duties? How do you think they differ from those of a Roman town official? You will find out at your local library or town hall.

2  Many Romans moved to live in another country in the hope of a better life. Imagine that you are a Roman girl or boy who has gone to Britain with their family to live. Write a letter to an old friend in Rome telling them about the differences.

3  Look at the map of Europe (a medieval copy of a Roman map). Why do you think it looks so different from a modern map?

## CAN YOU REMEMBER ?

*What was the main reason why provincial people disliked the Romans?*
*How did the building of good roads make Roman government easier?*
*Why was citizenship prized?*
*In what ways did the foundation of new towns help to spread the Roman way of life?*

## CHECK YOUR UNDERSTANDING

Can you remember the meaning of the following?

citizenship       forum
corruption       veteran

# Pax Romana (The Roman Peace)

There have been many European empires, including the Spanish, the Dutch, the German, the French and the British. Aelius Aristides, lecturing in Rome about the year 150 AD, said of the Roman Empire:

> The whole world speaks in unison . . . and so well does it harmonize . . . that it joins in praying this Empire may last for all time.

A Greek writer wrote:

> The greatest blessings that cities can enjoy are peace, prosperity, populousness and concord. As far as peace is concerned the people have no need of political activity, for all war, both Greek and foreign, has been banished and has disappeared from among us. Of liberty the people enjoy as much as our rules allow them, and perhaps more would not be better.

> (Plutarch, *Precepts of Statecraft*, XXXII)

In contrast with the views of the writers above, this is what Tacitus, a Roman historian, wrote about British feelings when Agricola was governor from 78–85 AD. (Conscription is compulsory enlistment for military service.)

> Among the many British war chiefs was one named Calgacus, who was pre-eminent in valour and in birth. He is reported to have addressed in the following manner the assembled crowd of Britons, who were clamouring for battle, 'Nature has planned that each man love his children and family very dearly. Yet these are torn from us by conscription to be slaves elsewhere . . . Our possessions and our money are consumed in paying tribute; our farmland and our yearly produce are consumed in providing them with grain; our very bodies and hands are worn down while clearing forests and swamps for them, who beat and insult us.

> (Tacitus, *Agricola* 29–31)

The writer suggests that the people of the Empire enjoyed only limited liberty. What freedoms do you think are important?
Plutarch's and Calgacus' were two very different views of Roman government. Why is this?
If Tacitus, a Roman, records Calgacus' words, how do we rate him as a historian?

*Romanization had its brutal side. In this relief a defiant barbarian fights back against a legionary.*

The Roman Empire owed its existence to the supremacy of its army. Every year, before 107 BC, the two consuls called all land-owning citizens between the ages of 17 and 46 to the Capitoline Hill above Rome, where the military tribunes chose the soldiers they needed. Pay was very little, each man had to provide his own equipment and when the campaign was over, soldiers returned to their homes.

After this time, as the Empire grew bigger, a full-time permanent army became a necessity, and men without property were allowed to enlist. When they left the army after twenty years service they were given money and land. Later still, men who were not Roman citizens were able to join. They were called *auxiliaries*, and when they retired were given citizenship. *Numeri* were regiments of tribespeople from outside the Empire, who were used to defend distant frontiers. These people were very seldom made citizens.

Life in the army was hard, and discipline was strict. You could be put to death for sleeping on guard, and for cowardice in battle a unit might be *decimated*, that is, every tenth soldier put to death. Lesser crimes would be punished by stoppage of pay or a reduction in seniority.

The army was organised into *legions*. Each legion consisted of approximately 5,000 men divided into ten *cohorts*, and each cohort was divided into *centuries*, which despite their name consisted of eighty men under the command of *centurions*. The backbone of the army was the *legionary*, the ordinary foot soldier. He wore a leather tunic and sandals in summer, and in cold weather, leggings, a cloak and strong boots. His weapons were swords, daggers, and javelins, and for protection he wore a metal helmet, an oblong, slightly curved shield over his tunic, and on the lower part of his legs armour called *greaves*. When advancing he carried a change of clothing, spare boots, enough food for three days, a cooking pot, a spade, a saw and two fencing posts – a combined weight of over forty kilos.

Chester's fort and Hadrian's Wall.

A reconstruction of Roman fortifications at Alesia, south-west France.

Many legionaries were skilled craftsmen such as stonemasons, carpenters, engineers, and surveyors, and their skills were particularly useful in the building of roads, bridges and aqueducts, an important part of the army's work. Every legion also contained doctors, vets, musicians and cavalry (horsemen), who acted as despatch carriers and scouts.

A legionary's immediate superior was the *centurion*. His armour was heavier, he wore a leather tunic, and his helmet had a red plume, so that he could be easily seen. He carried as a badge of office a stick, made from a vine stem, with which he could beat his men. The commander of a legion was the *legate* and below him were senior and junior *tribunes*. The camp prefect was in charge of training and equipment. He had usually been a centurion who had served for thirty years. The *aquilifer* carried the standard of the legion, the eagle, and the *signifer* carried the standard of the century.

Much territory was captured not in pitched battle, but by besieging key towns in an area, and the Romans developed several weapons that were of particular use for this. They had mobile towers, that could be wheeled right up to the walls of the besieged town. There were huge battering rams, manned by 20 or 30 men. A massive stone-throwing machine, an *onager* could hurl a boulder weighing 30 kilos almost half a mile, while the *ballista*, a huge crossbow, fired bolts at the enemy walls. Soldiers attacking on foot often protected themselves from stones being hurled at them by locking together their shields over their heads. They called this a *testudo* (tortoise).

Josephus, a Jewish priest writing in the first century AD, describes Roman soldiers going to war 'all marching silently and in good order'. Their discipline, training and weaponry made them a formidable war-machine.

## A Soldier's Pay

Soldiers had to pay for their own food and clothing. Here is an extract from an account from 81 AD of a cavalryman of a legion stationed outside Alexandria in Egypt. It was found on a piece of papyrus. We do not know who Rennius Innocens was. Perhaps he was a centurion.

| Received third salary payment for year | | 248 drachmas |
| --- | --- | --- |
| Deductions | Hay | 10 drachmas |
| | Towards rations | 80 drachmas |
| | Boots and leggings | 12 drachmas |
| | Towards clothing | 146 drachmas |
| Total expenses | | 248 drachmas |

**(Verified by Rennius Innocens)**

This cavalryman's expenses against his first two payments were 288 drachmas, so that out of total pay for the year of 744 drachmas, he was given 208 drachmas, approximately 30 per cent of what he earned.

## Compulsory Saving

Although a soldier actually received such a small proportion of what he earned, even then he wasn't able to do what he liked with it.

> One half of the monies, which the soldiers obtained were kept in a safe place, lest it be squandered by them in luxuries, and the purchase of useless things ... The soldier, who knows that his money is kept here entertains no thoughts of desertion, cherishes the standards more and fights for them in the line with greater bravery.
>
> **(Vegetius, *Military Science*)**

Vegetius' book on the Roman army has, until modern times, been regarded by the military as a classic handbook on how an army should be organised and soldiers trained. Vegetius wrote in the fourth and fifth centuries, and is describing the army of an earlier period. There was also a bag, kept by the standard-bearer, to which every soldier contributed for burial expenses.

**Why do you think this bag was entrusted to the standard-bearer?**

**Do you think all these deductions were fair?**

*Parts of a soldier's armour.*

*Each legion had an* aquilifer *to carry the eagle standard into battle.*

## Building a Bridge

Cassio Dio was a distinguished senator who wrote in the third century AD. Here he describes how the Romans solved the problem of crossing wide, deep rivers.

River channels are abridged with great ease, since the soldiers are always practising this operation on the Danube, the Rhine and the Euphrates. Now the method is as follows. The boats are flat-bottomed and are anchored a little way upstream from where the bridge is to be constructed. They first let one ship drift downstream close to the bank that they are holding; and when it has come opposite the spot that is to be bridged, they throw into the stream a wicker basket filled with stones and fastened by a cable, that serves as an anchor. By means of planks, a floor is at once laid to the landing place. Then they send down another ship at a little distance from the first, and another one beyond that, until they have extended the bridge to the opposite bank. The ship that is nearest the enemy's bank carries towers upon it, and a gate, archers and catapults.

(Cassio Dio, *Roman History*)

## THINGS TO DO

1  One of the most famous sieges the Romans conducted was that of Masada (now in modern Israel). Look up Masada in an encyclopedia, and read its story.
2  Roman soldiers fought in lines about two metres apart. When men in the front row fell, those in the row behind stepped into their place. Why did the Romans fight like this? Can you think of other fighting formations (on the North American frontier, for example)?
3  Look at the picture of a reconstructed Roman fort on page 17. If you were attacking the fort, how would you try to get past these defences?

## CAN YOU REMEMBER ?

*Why did the Romans need a permanent army?*
*For what reasons was sleeping on guard duty regarded as a serious crime?*
*How important is good discipline in an army?*
*What was the purpose of the plume in a centurion's helmet?*
*What did the legionary carry when the army was on the move?*

Can you think of any problems with building a bridge in this way? What would towers be used for?

## CHECK YOUR UNDERSTANDING

Can you remember the meaning of the following?

| | |
|---|---|
| ballista | legate |
| decimated | numeri |

# PROSPERITY

Money and goods flowed into Rome in the form of taxation and booty from conquered peoples, but the first two centuries of the Roman Empire were particularly prosperous ones for many of the provinces as well, despite the payments to Rome. We can see their prosperity in the remains of their cities. To take two examples, Nîmes and Ephesus. Nîmes in Gaul (present day France) has a large amphitheatre (still used for bull-fights) a three-tiered aqueduct over the river Gard, and a beautiful temple; and Ephesus (in present day Turkey) had an amphitheatre that could seat twenty-four thousand spectators.

Agriculture and trade were able to flourish for a number of reasons. The Roman army maintained stability, and farmers could cultivate their fields in peace. Soldiers needed great quantities of food, clothing and weapons, and supplying these gave work to many people. More money came into circulation. The creation of new towns provided market places, where goods could be bought and sold. The building of thousands of miles of well-paved roads made travel easier, and sea routes were made safe from the attacks of pirates.

Very cheap labour was supplied by a huge number of slaves. Julius Caesar, for example, is said to have enslaved more than a million people during his period in Gaul from 58 to 51 BC. This figure may not be accurate, but it is clear that very large numbers were concerned.

Although most trade was local, that is, people taking their produce or goods to the nearest market, Rome remained the centre of economic life of the Empire as a whole. Goods were generally transported there by sea, because it was cheaper than by land. To help trade the Emperor Claudius greatly enlarged Ostia, the port of Rome, and linked it to the river Tiber by canal. From Egypt came great quantities of corn, sufficient to feed Rome itself for four months a year, and glass, textiles, and papyrus. Syria sent wine, dried fruit and spice. Asia Minor supplied olive oil, wine, fruit, salted fish, silks, carpets and woollen goods. From Gaul there was wine, olive oil, glass and pottery. Spain was rich in minerals and sent gold, silver, lead and iron, as well as corn, oil and wine.

In Rome itself we have evidence of large brick yards; much of the brick used at Ostia was carried there along the river Tiber. Another Italian brickyard was on the northern coast of the Adriatic Sea near Rimini. Metalwork was an important industry both in Rome and the rest of Italy. In Rome along the Via Sacra (Sacred Way) from inscriptions we know that there were two goldsmiths, an engraver and a maker of silver. Aquileia, at the head of the Adriatic, was the centre of an iron industry; Capua was noted for its copper work.

Pottery was made in great quantities in Italy and traded all over the Empire. Most of it was produced to provide containers for the storage and carriage of food and wine. Some of these jars, called amphorae, were very large indeed, and could hold over a thousand litres. Samian ware with its red, glossy surface was very popular for use at table. This was first made at Arezzo in Italy and had a very large export market. Italy was also rich in agricultural produce, and its wine and olive oil were prized in many parts of the Empire.

There was much trade with countries beyond the Empire, too. Under the Emperor Nero, the amber route to the eastern Baltic came under Roman control. From the east coast of Africa came ivory, rhinoceros horn, tortoiseshell, palm oil, cinnamon, frankincense, and slaves. India's main exports were peppers, spices, jewels and cloth, and it acted as a trading post for silk from China.

Landowners and traders grew rich at this time and shopkeepers and skilled craftsmen did well, but it seems unlikely that most labourers shared the general prosperity. In the time of Augustus 300,000 people in Rome, a third of the population, was receiving the corn dole, free supplies of corn. Sometimes, if it came late, there were riots. For peasants in the countryside there was a barely adequate standard of living. Slaves, although their treatment probably depended on how valuable their skills were to their masters, were often treated very badly. The benefits of a thriving economy were, therefore, enjoyed by only a very small section of society as a whole.

(Above) *Unloading a cargo ship.*

*A painting of the elaborate and prosperous harbour of Ostia at the mouth of the Tiber river.*

## Slavery

Much of the labour of farms and factories was supplied by slaves, of whom there was a very great number. Many of them were captured in war and many were the children of slaves. Both men and women could also be enslaved for debt or crime, and children were sometimes sold by families who could no longer feed them. Household slaves were often much better treated than farm or mine slaves, although even here treatment very much depended on the temperament of owners. Here is an example of the worst treatment, that of slaves in the Spanish silver mines, by a Greek historian living in the first century AD.

They are given no rest or break from their toil, but rather are forced by the whiplashes of their overseers to endure the most dreadful of hardships ... although they often pray more for death than for life because of the magnitude of their suffering.

(Diodorus of Sicily, *The History of the World*)

Seneca, a philosopher of the first century AD, reveals a more humane attitude.

I was happy to learn, that you live on friendly terms with your slaves. This attitude is quite in keeping with your good sense and your liberal education. Some people say 'They're just slaves'. But they are fellow human beings. They live with us.

(Seneca the Younger, *Letters*)

**What benefits would owners gain by treating their slaves well?**

*Second century relief of a ship carrying wine barrels.*

## THINGS TO DO

1 Imagine you are a slave working on a large agricultural estate. The owner makes an unexpected visit, he speaks to you, and you plead for freedom for yourself and your family. What arguments do you use to persuade him?

2 Study the picture of Julius' house above. Make a plan of a similar villa, showing all the activities that you would expect to see on a typical Roman estate.

## CHECK YOUR UNDERSTANDING

Can you remember the meaning of the following?

amphorae     corn dole
booty     procurator

*Activities on a country estate including hunting, olive harvesting and offering fowl and produce to the landowner.*

## Estate Management

The Emperor was by far the biggest landowner in the Empire. Usually, an imperial estate was administered by a *procurator*, who leased land to tenant farmers, who themselves sometimes sublet. Some tenants had to hand over a share of the crops, and give a certain number of days of labour in return for their lands. Others were charged a rent they could pay in goods. Large estates grew at the expense of small. Pliny in his *Natural History* says six owners were in possession of one half of the province of Africa at the time of the Emperor Nero. Columella, writing in the first century, gives this advice:

> **The master must give special attention, among other things, to labourers . . . He should be civil in dealing with the tenant farmers, should show himself affable, and should be more exacting in the matter of work than of payments . . . For when land is carefully tilled, it usually brings a profit, and never a loss, except when it is assailed by unusually severe weather or robbers.**
>
> **(Columella, *On Agriculture*)**

**Why are large estates more economic to run than small ones?**

## The Grain Fleet

Lucian, who lived in the second century AD, wrote this description of a ship, which carried grain from Egypt to Ostia.

> **What a big ship! About 180ft (60 metres) long, a ship builder would say . . . and the maximum depth from deck to keel, about 44ft (14 metres) . . . And how the stern rises with its gentle curve, with its gilded beak, balanced at the opposite end by the long rising extension of the prow with a figure of the name-goddess of the ship, Isis, on either side. As to the other ornamental details, the paintings and the fiery bright topsail . . . The size of the crew could be compared to that of an army. And they were saying that she carried enough grain to feed everybody in Attica for a year . . .**
>
> **(Lucian, *The Ship*)**

A ship of this size would probably carry about 1300 tonnes of grain. Its keel is the long piece of timber on which its frame is built. The stern is the back of a ship, and the prow its front.

## CAN YOU REMEMBER ?

*How do we know that many of the provinces grew rich at this time?*
*Why were agriculture and trade able to flourish?*
*What goods came from Egypt?*
*Who enlarged the port of Ostia, and how did he link it to Rome?*

# ROME

The prosperity of the Empire, although of little comfort for many of its inhabitants, meant that the emperors were able to accumulate huge sums of money from taxation and captured treasure, much of which was spent on lavish building projects in the imperial capital of Rome.

Every town of any size had a *forum*, a large open space, surrounded by the lawcourts and offices, where people met to talk and do business. The Forum Romanum was the most famous of all with a marker in the middle from which every milestone on every road was measured – you may have heard the saying 'all roads lead to Rome'. Julius Caesar began the building of a magnificent new forum for the city. He finished a Senate House begun by Sulla, and built a beautiful temple, dedicated to Venus.

In his *Res Gestae* (*Achievements*) Augustus boasted, 'I left Rome a city of marble, though I found it only a city of bricks'. His chief monument was the temple of Jupiter on the Capitoline Hill, which he decorated with seven tons of gold and jewels. The Emperor Nero built the Golden House, a vast, luxurious palace, surrounded by lakes and parks. After Nero's suicide a huge amphitheatre holding 70,000 spectators was built in the grounds. We call it the Colosseum, because a colossal statue of Nero once stood there. Two military monuments were the Arch built by the Emperor Titus to commemorate the defeat of the Jewish revolt in 73 AD, and the Column built by Trajan in 113 AD to signal his conquest of Dacia.

Another famous landmark was the Circus Maximus, the home of horse-racing and later chariot-racing. It was enclosed by walls about fifteen metres high, and could seat 150,000 people.

Only the rich had bathrooms in their own houses, and very many Romans used the public baths. There were over nine hundred of these public

baths by 300 AD. They varied greatly in size and opulence. Those of the Emperor Caracalla were approximately two hundred by one hundred metres, were richly decorated with marble, precious stones and mosaics, and were surrounded by other sporting facilities. Baths consisted of a series of rooms and pools, a hot, dry room, a cool room, a room of moderate temperature and a hot, steamy room.

More than 1,000 million litres of water were brought into Rome daily from nearby hills by water-carrying channels, most of which were underground, but in order to cross a valley or a ravine, some had to be built on bridges supported by arches. The sixty-four kilometre long Aqua Claudia, built by the Emperor Claudius, is a very beautiful example of this. One aqueduct, the Aqua Alsietina, sent all its waters to a special amphitheatre that could be flooded for water shows.

Magnificent as many of Rome's public buildings were, the vast majority of Rome's inhabitants, about a million of them by the time of Augustus, lived in filthy and squalid conditions in high-rise blocks of flats called *insulae* (islands). Most insulae were very badly built. Because land was expensive, landlords tended to build higher and higher blocks on foundations that were far too small. Buildings frequently collapsed, and Augustus finally forbade private individuals to erect any structure more than twenty metres high. Another cause of collapse was the flimsiness of the walls. These were often made of mud and wattle (branches of trees), which dried out and crumbled in the summer heat. The massive wooden beams, which shored up the floors, added to the risk of fire. Rooms, if they were heated at all, were heated by charcoal braziers, and lit by torches or candles, and outbreaks of fire were an everyday occurrence. Augustus created a corps of fire-fighting night watchmen, called *vigiles*, but most Romans lived in dread.

There was no water in the insulae: it had to be carried upstairs in clay jars or goatskins from a public fountain. Some insulae had lavatories in the basement, but most people used public ones. Imperial Rome is aptly described by the phrase 'public affluence (meaning wealth) and private squalor'.

(Left) *The* Forum Romanum.

*The Colosseum, finished in 80 AD, held 70,000 spectators.*

## All Roads Lead to Rome

The city of Rome has always been recognized as one of the most beautiful cities in the world. One name that it has been given is 'The Eternal City'. A fourth-century writer describes how the Emperor Constantine saw it in 357 AD.

> So then Constantinus entered Rome, the home of empire and of every virtue, and when he had come to the Rostra, the most renowned forum of ancient dominion he stood amazed; and on every side on which his eyes rested he was dazzled by the array of marvellous sights . . . But when he came to the Forum of Trajan, a construction unique under the heaven as we believe, and admirable even in the unanimous opinion of the gods, he stood fast in amazement, turning his attention to the gigantic complex about him, beggaring description and never again to be imitated by mortal men.
>
> (Ammianus Marcellinus, *History*, XVI. X13–15)

A Rostrum was a speaker's platform on the Forum. Compare this passage to the words of Juvenal, writing in the first century AD.

> Who at cool Praeneste, or at Volsinii amid its leafy hills, was ever afraid of his house tumbling down? . . . But here we inhabit a city propped up for the most part by slats (a narrow strip of wood): for that is how the landlord patches up the crack in the old wall, bidding the inmates sleep at ease under the ruin that hangs above their heads.

With these two very different views on the architecture of Rome, what do you think a town or city needs in order to be a good place to live?

## CHECK YOUR UNDERSTANDING

Can you remember the meaning of the following?

aqueduct     forum
brazier      insulae

*Model of imperial Rome. The Colosseum is centre right.*

*Thermae at Herculaneum.*

## The Baths

The baths (thermae) were places where Romans went not only to bathe and swim, but to talk and meet their friends, to conduct business, and to enjoy many different sports and recreations. The entrance fee was a quadrans, a quarter of an ass, the smallest coin. Children entered free. In the centre of the thermae were the baths proper, and around them a covered walk. Behind this there might be a gymnasium, sitting-rooms, a library, and space for many different kinds of sporting activities. The baths described here were particularly luxurious ones. Lucian lived in the second century AD.

One is received into a public hall of good size with ample accommodation for servants and attendants... Next, capacious locker rooms to undress in... and three swimming pools of cold water... On leaving this hall you come into another which is slightly warmed... and next to it a very bright hall fitted up for massage... the hall beyond it is very beautiful, full of abundant light and aglow with colour like that of purple hangings. It contains three hot tubs... the bath is beautified with other marks of thoughtfulness – with two toilets, many exits, and two devices for telling time, a water clock that makes a bellowing sound and a sundial.

(Lucian, *Hippias* (or *the Bath*))

## THINGS TO DO

1 Lucian mentions a water clock at the baths. Can you find out how one works? (try an encyclopedia)

2 Imagine that you are the slave or servant of a rich man on one of his trips to the baths. Give an account of what your master expects you to do for him there. Remember that the Romans didn't have soap; they used a strigil, an instrument with a sharp blade to scrape themselves clean. (Slaves were often very well-educated.)

## CAN YOU REMEMBER ?

*Why were the walls of the insulae sometimes not very safe?*

*How did most people obtain their water?*

*Why was the Colosseum given its name?*

*What was special about the Aqua Alsietina?*

# RELIGION AND EDUCATION

Many of the most beautiful buildings in Rome were temples, each dedicated to a particular god or goddess. There was the temple of Diana, the goddess of women and children, the temple of Venus, the goddess of love, the temple of Apollo, the god of art, music and beauty, and many more besides. For the Romans religious worship was not a matter of personal belief, but more a contract with the gods. If they prayed and sacrificed, the gods in return would protect them. In general, the Romans were tolerant of the gods of countries they conquered as long as their own were worshipped as well. At Baalbek (Heliopolis) in Syria, for example, the sanctuary, the inner room of the temple, has a joint dedication to Jupiter and to Baal, the most important of the local gods.

In time, the emperors themselves began to be worshipped, possibly to encourage loyalty and to provide a religious focus for the Empire as a whole. At Lyon in present-day France, an altar was dedicated to Augustus and Rome, and at Colchester in Britain, a very large temple was built and dedicated to the Emperor Claudius.

The second and third centuries AD saw great changes in religious practice. Greater ease of communication meant that new ideas could spread more quickly, and worship of the Egyptian gods Isis and Osiris and the Persian god Mithras became popular. These new mystery religions, so-called because there were secret rites for new members, differed from ancient forms of worship in that they were based on personal conviction, and offered not only protection but a direct relationship with god and an explanation of suffering and wickedness.

Another important religion that took hold at the beginning of the Empire was Christianity. Its name comes from the title Christ (a Greek word meaning the anointed one) given to Jesus of Nazareth. Christians believe that he was sent by God and that there is only one God. After Jesus' crucifixion by the Romans in about 33 AD, his followers tried to spread as widely as possible his and their ideas about God, life after death and how a good life should be lived. Because they refused to worship the Roman gods they were often persecuted by the Roman authorities. Not all emperors were intolerant of them, but many Christians were killed in the first three centuries, and it was not until the conversion of the Emperor Constantine in 312 AD, when he attributed his victory over his rival Maxentius to his vision of the Christian cross, that Christianity became accepted. When the Emperor Theodosius banned other religions, Christianity became the official religion of the Empire.

Part of the attraction of Christianity was the message of equality to rich and poor alike. As far as education was concerned, there was vast inequality.

There was no system of state schooling in the Empire, although individual cities employed

teachers. We have a letter of Pliny the Younger, for example, in which he described how he tried to set up a council in Como to organize a city school. Some rich families had private tutors. There were three kinds of schools for those who could afford them. For the youngest, both boys and girls, the subjects taught were reading, writing, and numberwork, and children were also expected to learn by heart chunks of poetry, laws and legends.

Girls finished with school at the age of ten or eleven and many boys went out to work. For those boys who continued their education the curriculum included Greek, philosophy, poetry, music and natural science. At fourteen or fifteen a very few went on to the third school to study public speaking, law and politics. For the richest a tour of foreign countries might follow.

Books were rare, and waxed tablets were usually used to write on. The writer used a sharp-pointed instrument called a *stilus* to scratch words on the wax. The other end of the stilus was blunt and could be used for smoothing over the wax. Classes usually started at daybreak and went on till noon. Sometimes they were held in the open air, in open spaces, or even on the pavement to save teachers paying rent for classrooms.

(Left) *The education of Dionysus: this wall painting shows the life of the Greek god, worshipped in Rome as Bacchus.*

*The Pantheon (the temple of all the gods) was built in Rome between 118 and 125 AD. This is the finest building of the Roman world to have survived in its original form.*

# RELIGION AND EDUCATION

## Papyrus

Most official writing in the ancient world was done on papyrus. This is an account of how it was made, written in the first century AD.

> Papyrus grows in the marshes of Egypt, or in the sluggish waters of the Nile . . . The root has the thickness of a man's arm; the stalk is triangular and tapers gracefully upward to a height of not more than about fifteen feet . . . The various kinds of paper are processed upon a board moistened with Nile water, the muddy liquid of which has the effect of glue. First an upright layer is spread upon the board, the full length of the papyrus being used . . . after which cross strips are used, producing a lattice work effect. Next, the sheets are pressed with presses, and then dried in the sun; after which they are joined together.

**(Pliny, *Natural History*)**

Some people also wrote on vellum, which was made from the skins of young animals. It was very much more expensive than papyrus.

**Though better than wax tablets, papyrus had some disadvantages. Can you think what they were?**

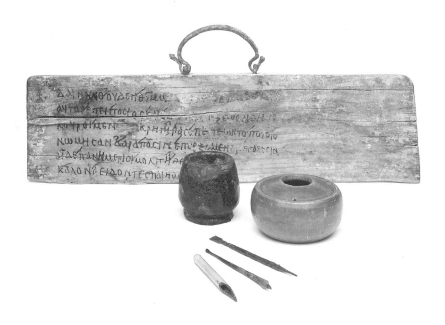

*One of four ivory panels with scenes from the events of Christ's crucifixion.*

*Writing implements – stiluses, reed pens and inkpots.*

## CAN YOU REMEMBER?

*Why were mystery religions so called? In what ways did they differ from older forms of worship? To what did Constantine attribute his victory over Maxentius?*
*What was used for writing in schools?*
*Why did ideas begin to spread more quickly?*

## Persecution

In 64 AD a great fire destroyed a large part of Rome, and many people believed that Nero himself was responsible. This is how Nero defended himself:

> But the terrible rumour that Nero himself had ordered the burning of Rome could not be quelled by charitable distributions or donations... Therefore Nero sought to put down the rumour by providing culprits, and visited with outrageous punishments a group called Christians... They took their name from a certain Christus, who had been punished with death by the procurator Pontius Pilate in the reign of Tiberius... Mockery was heaped upon them as they were killed: wrapped in the skins of wild animals, they were torn apart by dogs, or nailed to crosses, or set on fire and burned alive to provide light at night.
>
> (Tacitus, *Annals*)

## Judaism

There were Jews living in many parts of the Empire. They did not try to persuade other people to adopt their ideas as Christians did, but they wanted to remain a separate community, and they refused to worship Roman gods. In this letter written in 41 AD Emperor Claudius urges the people of Alexandria in Egypt to be tolerant.

> Therefore I entreat you, the Alexandrians, to behave tolerantly and benevolently toward the Jews, since they have lived in the same city as you for many years, and to allow them to observe their own customs... For I, having heard both sides, have approved these customs. But without reservation I order the Jews not to agitate for more indulgence than they enjoyed in the past, and not to send in the future a second, separate delegation, as if they lived in a separate city.
>
> (From a Greek papyri in the British Museum)

What reason might Nero have had for starting a great fire in Rome? Why would it have spread so quickly?

### THINGS TO DO

1 The Romans had many gods. Some were worshipped for particular reasons. Make a list of their names and why they were worshipped.

2 Roman emperors were often worshipped as gods. See if you can find out if any modern leaders have been treated as gods.

3 Find out about the Roman system of numbers. (It's very different to the Arabic system of numbers we use.) What other number systems can you discover?

What reasons does Claudius give for toleration?

### CHECK YOUR UNDERSTANDING

Can you remember the meaning of the following?

curriculum          stilus
sanctuary           tolerant

*These silver plaques combine pagan beliefs with a Christian symbol – chi-rho.*

# FAMILY LIFE

Most marriages were arranged ones, that is the parents decided who their children were to marry rather than allowing them to choose for themselves. At engagement a girl was given a ring and presents. She was usually married between the ages of thirteen and seventeen, and her husband would be a little older. At her wedding the girl wore a tunic without a hem, a yellow cloak, yellow sandals, and over her hair a flame-coloured veil and a wreath of flowers.

The ceremony began with an animal sacrifice to see if its entrails predicted the success of the marriage. If all was well the couple exchanged simple vows, witnesses put their seal to the wedding contract, and then the celebrations began. There was much feasting and singing, and a procession through the streets to the bride's new home.

If a bride's family was comfortably off, it was the custom that she should bring with her a dowry, that is a gift from her family of money and possessions. According to one marriage contract the bridegroom promised 'to furnish her with all the necessities and clothing according to his means.' If he did not do this he agreed to return the dowry. During Imperial

times it was usual for a married woman to keep control of the property she owned before her marriage. The vast majority of Romans, of course, had very little to bring by way of a dowry.

Roman fathers had complete control over their children, and until 374 AD could abandon new-born babies they did not want or could not afford (it was called exposing them). These were often sick children, or girls, who would not be able to support themselves or who might need a dowry. Discipline in the home was strict and in the case of divorce, which was relatively easy, the children remained with their fathers not their mothers. Many women died young in childbirth, while a man might marry two or three times. Having children was considered very commendable, and a woman with three children was entitled to wear a special tunic.

Children who were orphaned could have a very difficult time. If they belonged to a richer family there would probably be someone who would care for them, but for poorer children there were no state homes. Some emperors made money available for welfare assistance, and from time to time wealthy people endowed charities. Adoption took place, not always of orphans. Sometimes parents could not afford to feed their children, and they preferred to give them away rather than to see them starve.

Most people in Italian cities lived in dark, insanitary tenement blocks with neither water nor heating. In contrast, the houses of the wealthy were often very luxurious. They were built around a courtyard or a garden, and had dining-rooms, bedrooms, kitchens, bathrooms and a covered verandah. They also had sanitation and an under-floor central heating system called a *hypocaust*. The floors of rooms that were to be heated were supported by short pillars. Hot air from a furnace circulated around these pillars, and then up to the rooms above through ducts built in the walls.

This type of house was increasingly copied throughout the empire, and in the country was often a farm as well. It was called a villa. But just as in Rome most people lived in squalor, so in the rest of the Empire poor people remained in very simple houses with thatched roofs and walls made of branches packed with mud.

Atrium of a house at Herculaneum.

A Roman marriage. Clasping hands
means that a couple is now married. The
man is holding a wedding contract
drawn up before the ceremony.

Dishes prepared for a banquet: a gazelle,
fowl, vegetables and fruit.

*A loaf preserved in the volcanic ash that covered Pompeii.*

## Giving Away a Child

This official document was written in Egypt in 554 AD.

My husband died and I was left, to toil and suffer for my daughter by him, to provide her with the barest necessities of life. And now I no longer have the means to feed her . . . She is now about nine years old. I have requested that you receive her from me as your daughter and I acknowledge that I have handed her over to you from now and forever as your legal daughter . . . And I acknowledge that I have no power henceforth to reclaim her from you.

**Why do you think this document is so carefully worded?**

## Food

The main meal of the Roman day was eaten late in the afternoon or early evening. The chief food of poorer people was a kind of porridge, bread and vegetables. The writer Cato suggested that slaves be given wheat or bread, figs, discarded olives and the dregs of fish sauce. A good dinner would consist of three courses, a first course of eggs, cheese, vegetables, salt fish, shell fish or possibly dormice, the main course of boiled or roasted meat, with wine, and finally fruit and sweets. Spices were frequently used, not just for their flavour, but to disguise the taste of food going bad. Some rich people lived very extravagantly indeed, and ate delicacies such as peacocks, cranes, swordfish, oysters and young kids. There were no forks and people ate mainly with their fingers. Here is a recipe for rabbit with fruit sauce from the first century.

Cook the rabbit in wine, liquamen (a liquid obtained from salted fish) with a little bit of mustard, anise (a plant from the Middle East) and a whole leek. When the rabbit is done, prepare this sauce: pepper, onion ring, dates, two damson plums, wine, liquamen and a small amount of olive oil. Thicken with starch and allow the mixture to boil for a short time. Pour this sauce over the rabbit in a serving dish.

**(Apicius, *Cookbook*)**

**We have some very great advantages over the Romans in the preparation and preservation of food. What are they?**

*A group of boys playing knucklebones.*

## Choosing a Husband

Pliny, who was born in either 61 or 62 AD, was a very distinguished lawyer and administrator. We have 247 of his personal letters, and 121 official ones to and from the Emperor Trajan. They give a very good picture of upper-class Roman life at the turn of the first century.

**To Junius Maurias:**

**You ask me to look for a husband for your brother's daughter . . . I should have had a long search if Minicius Acilianus were not at hand . . . His native place is Brixia, one of the towns in our part of Italy, which still retains intact much of its honest simplicity . . . You will find nothing to criticize in the whole household. Acilianus himself has abundant energy and application, but no lack of modesty . . . He has a frank expression, and his complexion is fresh and high-coloured; his general good looks have a natural nobility . . . I am wondering whether to add that his father has ample means . . . Certainly if one thinks of the children of the marriage, and subsequent generations, the question of money must be taken into account.**

**(Pliny the Younger, *Letter 14*)**

## THINGS TO DO

1  There are many Roman villas in England. Try to visit one of them. Chedworth villa near Cirencester is a particularly fine example.
2  The dowry system was customary in many countries until relatively recently, and some still have it. Use your local library to find out more about it. What are its advantages and disadvantages?

## CHECK YOUR UNDERSTANDING

Can you remember the meaning of the following?

liquamen      dowry
contract      entrails

## CAN YOU REMEMBER ?

*At what age were girls usually married?*
*What similarities are there between Roman wedding clothes and those worn at church weddings today?*
*Why did many women die young?*
*What kind of central heating did wealthy Romans have?*

Would you trust Pliny's recommendation? What else might we look for in an ideal husband?

From an early date the rulers of Rome realized the importance of keeping the people entertained. If people were contented they were very much less likely either to fight amongst themselves or to try to overthrow the government. In one year alone of Augustus' reign there were sixty-five days of games of different kinds.

Chariot-racing was very popular indeed, and the largest venue for it was the Circus Maximus in Rome, which was begun by Julius Caesar, and developed by later emperors. The track was approximately two hundred metres long, and the stands which surrounded it could hold more than 150,000 people. The chariot, a two-wheeled cart, was usually drawn by teams of four horses, although up to ten could be used. The course was seven times around the circus, and normally there were twenty-four races a day. There were four competitors in each race, representing the white, green, blue and red teams, and spectators then were just as enthusiastic about the teams they supported as football fans are today. Horse racing and acrobatic shows also took place at the Circus Maximus.

The Flavian Amphitheatre, which we call the Colosseum, was the main theatre for fights. The writer Martial tells us of tigers pitted against lions, rhinoceros against bulls and bulls against elephants. But what the people liked best was when the gladiators fought, either against animals or against themselves. Gladiators were often either criminals, prisoners-of-war or slaves, but there were also professional fighters, trained in special schools, and they fought until one of them was either killed or so badly wounded that he could not carry on. The winner received gold or silver pieces, and a palm, and sometimes a golden bowl or a crown. The president of the games usually left it to the crowd to decide what should happen to the loser, if he was still alive. If the crowd thought he had fought well and deserved to live they raised their thumbs. Thumbs down meant death, and the wounded man was killed where he lay.

More than seventy amphitheatres used for animal and gladiatorial contests are known in the Roman world, some of the most impressive being at Arles and Nîmes in present-day France, Trier in what is now Germany, and Alexandria in Egypt.

Another entertainment was the staging of naval battles, where large numbers of gladiators fought at sea. Both Claudius and Augustus did this, and in 52 AD Claudius arranged a fight on the Fucine Lake between two fleets of nineteen thousand men each.

There were three theatres in Rome, the largest of which could seat twelve thousand people. Plays were of two main types, comedy with standard characters, such as the old man, the glutton (a very greedy person) and the fool, and a sort of music hall. Some plays were recited, not acted. Readings of historical writings, poetry and speeches were also well attended, as was mime (acting without words).

Athletics, too, was very popular. A guild of professional athletes, like many sporting professionals today, toured the Empire competing at different games. Many became very wealthy, and enjoyed special privileges, including the right to obtain pensions from their native cities.

## Pompeii

In 79 AD Mount Vesuvius erupted, and the town of Pompeii was buried under a mountain of ash. When it was excavated in the nineteenth century, almost everything was preserved as it was when life came to an end. Here is an advertisement painted on the wall of a building:

> **The gladiatorial troop hired by Aulus Suettius Certius will fight in Pompeii on 3 May. There will also be a wild animal hunt. The awnings will be used.**

Awnings were coverings to protect spectators from the sun. Two graffiti read 'Celadus, the Thracian, makes all the girls sigh', and 'Crescens, the netfighter, holds the heart of all the girls'. A netfighter was a gladiator, armed only with a net and a trident (a three-pronged spear).

**Q**

**Pompeii is a perfect time capsule. There were twenty inns and one hundred and eighteen bars there. What does this tell us of the social habits of the Romans of the time?**

(Right) *A child's doll and glass and pottery marbles.*

*Chariot race in the Circus Maximus.*

## Saturnalia

Saturnalia was a seven-day festival named after Saturn, originally the god of agriculture. It took place every year beginning on 17 December. There was much unrestrained merry-making, people gave each other gifts, and for one day slaves were released from their duties. Statius, a poet, wrote in the first century

> **Now as the shades of night draw on, what commotion attends the scattering of largesse [giving out favours or money] . . . Here a crowd of buxom Lydian girls are clapping their hands, here tinkle the cymbals of Cadiz, there troops of Syrians are making uproar . . . Countless voices are raised to heaven, acclaiming the Emperor's Saturnalia festival.**
>
> **(Statius, *Silvae*)**

**Q**

**What does this passage tell us of Roman society at this time?**

## Other Pastimes

The Romans were fond of backgammon, chess and draughts, but they had a passion for gambling, so much so that it was strictly forbidden by the authorities except in the arena or at the circus, or at the festival of Saturnalia. They used knucklebones or dice for games of chance, simple games like 'heads or tails' or 'odds or evens' also being popular. Another guessing game in which bets were laid was micatio, when two players had to guess correctly the number of fingers their opponent raised. There is a Latin phrase to describe a man, whose honesty is beyond doubt;

**You could play micatio with him in the dark.**

## The Greatest Games

Nero was emperor from 54 AD to 68 AD, and paid for many lavish spectacles. The most extravagant were the 'Greatest Games'.

**Nero presented a large number of different types of entertainments, youth athletic meets, chariot races, theatrical performances and gladiatorial shows ... And throughout the entire period of the Greatest Games gifts were distributed among the people; every single day a thousand birds, all different kinds were given away, as well as numerous food baskets and vouchers for grain, clothing, gold, silver, precious stones, pearls, paintings, slaves, horses, mules, even for tamed wild animals, and finally for ships, apartment buildings and farms.**

(Suetonius, *Lives of the Caesars*)

Suetonius goes on to say:

**In one ballet Icarus fell, when he first tried his wings, crashed near the emperor's couch, and spattered Nero with blood.**

The legend of Icarus is that he was the son of the master-craftsman Daedalus, who built two sets of wings from feathers and wax to fly from Crete to Athens. Icarus flew too near the sun, the wax melted, and he fell to his death.

### CHECK YOUR UNDERSTANDING

Can you remember the meaning of the following?

gladiator    mime
glutton    awnings

### CAN YOU REMEMBER?

*How were the teams in the chariot race distinguished?*
*Who were the gladiators?*
*What were the rewards for the winner of a gladiatorial contest?*
*Which sportsmen might be granted a pension by their home city?*

Why did Nero make all these generous gifts? What were the birds for?
What side of Nero's character does Suetonius' story show?

# THE DECLINE OF THE EMPIRE

The size of the Roman Empire made it very difficult to govern. Despite the excellent roads along which the army could travel relatively quickly, frontiers were so long and so far from Rome that they were always vulnerable to attack from the many barbarian tribes. Augustus recognized this problem in the first century, and recommended that no more territory be conquered, but his advice was ignored, and for another hundred years more and more land was annexed. The Empire was at its greatest extent under the Emperor Trajan, who ruled from 98–117 AD.

His successor Hadrian was in immediate difficulty on several fronts, and to keep out the Picts and the Scots in northern Britain, he built a huge wall from the Solway Firth to the mouth of the river Tyne. In other countries he built chains of forts, but he found it impossible to hold Trajan's conquests in Asia Minor. From this time on, the imperial frontiers were under almost constant attack from barbarians, who fought amongst themselves as well as against the Romans. Later emperors allowed some of them to settle within Roman boundaries in return for help with defence.

But as well as pressures from outside, there was considerable unrest among the Roman people themselves. The wealth of the empire declined rapidly with the cost of war, and taxation was heavy. Trade became less lucrative [profitable] as previously safe trade routes were pillaged by robbers and pirates. There were plagues and poor harvests, and as the population grew smaller there

*Aspects of St Augustine's book* City of God – *a mosaic on the dome of the baptistry in Ravenna. Augustine, like other Romans, was horrified by the sack of Rome in 410 AD.*

*The* Pont du Gard, *a 270-metre-long aqueduct at Nimes in France.*

were fewer people to join the army and to pay taxes. Several emperors were cruel and corrupt, and it became increasingly frequent for legions to have to be withdrawn from the provinces to keep the peace at home. At the beginning of the third century Rome had twenty-three emperors in seventy years.

To try to stop the rot, in 285 AD the Emperor Diocletian, who afterwards retired to a beautiful palace in Split (now in Croatia) to grow cabbages, decided that the empire be divided, with the western half ruled from Milan and the eastern half from what is now Turkey. In 326 the Emperor Constantine began to build a new eastern capital in the Greek city of Byzantium, and called it Constantinople (present day Istanbul).

The fourth century, however, saw fierce attacks on many provinces of the empire, including Britain. By 410 AD when the Britons appealed to the Emperor Honorius for help against the Angles and the Saxons the situation in Rome itself was so bad that Honorius replied that he could do nothing. In the same year the capital was sacked by Alaric the Goth. In 429 the Vandals captured Carthage and the rest of the north African provinces and in 451 the Huns led by Attila invaded Gaul. In 455 Attila sacked Rome again and in 476 the last Roman Emperor, also called Romulus, was deposed. The eastern empire, called the Byzantine Empire, continued to exist for another thousand years until 1453, but after more than five hundred years, the Roman Empire of the west was destroyed.

# THE DECLINE OF THE EMPIRE

## Barbarian Allies?

With a huge empire to defend the Romans allowed men from conquered territory to join the army. Barbarians were also sometimes allowed to settle within the frontiers to help defend them, often with unfortunate results. Probus was Emperor during the second half of the third century.

**He took 16,000 [German] recruits, all of whom he scattered through the various provinces, incorporating bodies of 50 or 60 in the detachments or among the soldiers along the frontier, for he said that the aid the Romans received from barbarian auxiliaries must be felt but not seen . . . But when he had likewise brought over many from other tribes – that is Gepedians, Greu-thungians [Goths] and Vandals – they all broke faith . . . and roamed over well-nigh the entire world on foot or in ships and did no little damage to the glory of Rome.**

**(*Historia Augusta (Life of Probus*))**

**If you had been emperor, would you have placed the German recruits in small groups in several provinces rather than in a single army? The writer says that they should be 'felt but not seen'. Is this the real reason?**

## Lament for Rome

Saint Jerome (331–419 AD) was a scholar whose version of the Latin Bible became the commonly accepted translation known as the Vulgate.

**The Roman world is falling, and yet we hold our heads erect instead of bowing our necks . . . Last year [395 AD] the wolves not of Arabia, but from the far north – were let loose upon us from the distant crags of the Caucasus [mountains], and in a short time they overran whole provinces. How many monasteries did they capture, how many rivers were reddened with men's blood?**

**(Jerome, *Letters*, IX 16–17)**

The Caucasus mountains are in modern Georgia.

**What does St Jerome mean by 'wolves'?**

(Right) *The Emperor Constantine.*

*The Empire falls to hostile forces as depicted on this eighth century casket lid showing Germanic warriors attacking a homestead.*

## THINGS TO DO

1 Make a list of some of the things in our everyday lives that remind us that Britain was once a Roman province. Where do we see Roman numerals? Can you find the names of any Roman towns (they often end in -cester or -chester)? Is there a Roman road near where you live?

2 What can you find out about the fall of the eastern part of the Empire in 1453? It will be under Byzantium or Constantinople in an encyclopedia.

## Trouble in Africa

Another reason for the decline of the Empire was the corruption of its officials. Here is Ammianus, who was born in 330 AD, writing about Africa.

Africa from the very beginning of Valentinian's reign [364 AD] was badly ravaged by the madness of the barbarians, who made daring forays and were eager for wholesale bloodshed and robbery. This evil was increased by the slackness of the army and its greed for seizing the property of others; and especially by the conduct of the governor, Romanus by name. He was hated by many because of his savage nature, but especially for his haste to outdo the enemy in devastating the provinces . . . I shall declare openly that Valentinian . . . punished the smallest faults of the common soldiers with the greatest severity, while sparing those of higher ranks; so that these assumed that they had complete licence for their sins [could do what they wanted], and were aroused to shameful and monstrous crimes.

(Ammianus Marcellinus, *History*)

From this account how would you assess the morale of the ordinary Roman soldier fighting in Africa?

## CHECK YOUR UNDERSTANDING

Can you remember the meaning of the following?

annex          pillage
lucrative      decline

## Savage Tribesmen

These tribesmen lived in what is now Egypt.

All alike are warriors of equal rank, half-nude, clad in dyed cloak as far as the waist, ranging widely with the help of swift horses and slender camels in times of peace or of disorder. No man ever grasps a plow-handle or cultivates a tree, none seeks a living by tilling the soil, but they rove continually over wide and extensive tracts without a home, without fixed abodes or laws; they cannot long endure the same sky, nor does the sun of a single district ever content them.

(Ammianus Marcellinus *History*, XIV)

## CAN YOU REMEMBER ?

*Why did the size of the Roman Empire make it difficult to govern?*
*How did the Emperor Hadrian defend the frontier in Britain?*
*What other defensive strategy did he use?*
*What did the Emperor Diocletian do to try to make the Empire easier to rule?*
*Who began to build a new capital for the eastern part of the Empire?*

## What can you remember?

What were the duties of the governor of a Roman province?

Where was Carthage, and what was its importance to Rome?

Why was Augustus so powerful?

What were some of the advantages and disadvantages of living under Roman rule?

Who were the centurions? What did they wear?

How did the Romans bring large quantities of water into Rome?

Why is a good water supply important to the life of a city?

In what ways did the newer religions differ from the more ancient ones?

Most girls today would not have enjoyed living in Roman times. Why not?

What was the Roman army's contribution to the prosperity of the Empire?

The gladiatorial games were very popular. Why was this?

Do you think that the Romans themselves were to blame for the decline of their empire? Give reasons for your answer.

# TIME CHART

**BC**

| | |
|---|---|
| 753 | The foundation of Rome |
| 509 | Rome becomes a republic |
| 266 | Rome becomes supreme power in Italy |
| 264–241 | First Punic War (Rome versus Carthage) |
| 241 | The capture of Rome's first foreign province, Sicily. |
| 218–202 | Second Punic War – Hannibal invades Italy |
| 202 | Battle of Zama, Hannibal defeated by Roman general Scipio |
| 197 | Defeat of Philip of Macedon by Rome |
| 148 | Greece made a Roman province |
| 146 | Carthage destroyed by Rome |
| 133 | The province of Asia established |
| 70–19 | The lifespan of the poet Virgil |
| 55 | The first invasion of Britain by Julius Caesar |
| 54 | The second invasion of Britain by Julius Caesar |
| 49 | Caesar crosses the river Rubicon with his army in order to seize power in Rome |
| 49–44 | First civil war |
| 44 | Dictatorship of Julius Caesar. Assassination in the same year |
| 43–30 | Second civil war |
| 31 | Defeat of Mark Antony by Octavian at Battle of Actium |
| 27 BC–AD 14 | Rule of Octavian (later Emperor Augustus) |

**AD**

| | |
|---|---|
| c 1–33 | Life span of Jesus |
| c 10–64 | Life span of St Paul |
| 43 | The Emperor Claudius begins to conquer Britain |
| 54–68 | The rule of the Emperor Nero |
| 64 | The great fire of Rome, and persecution of Christians |
| 69 | The year of the four emperors |
| 79 | Mount Vesuvius erupts and Pompeii is buried under ash |
| 80 | The Colosseum is opened |
| 114 | The Emperor Trajan's conquests mark the furthest extent of the Roman Empire |
| 122 | The Emperor Hadrian builds a wall across the north of Britain |
| 251 | Invasion of the Empire by the Goths and other tribes |
| 285 | The division of the Empire by the Emperor Diocletian |
| 313 | The Emperor Constantine allows Christians freedom of worship |
| 330 | The Emperor Constantine builds a new capital city for the eastern Empire and calls it Constantinople |
| 395 | The Christian Emperor Theodosius bans other religions |
| 410 | The Goths sack Rome |
| 429 | The Vandals capture Carthage |
| 451 | Huns led by Attila invade Gaul |
| 455 | Attila plunders Rome |
| 476 | The last Emperor of Rome, also called Romulus, is deposed |
| 1453 | The capture of Constantinople by Ottoman Turks marks the end of the eastern Empire |

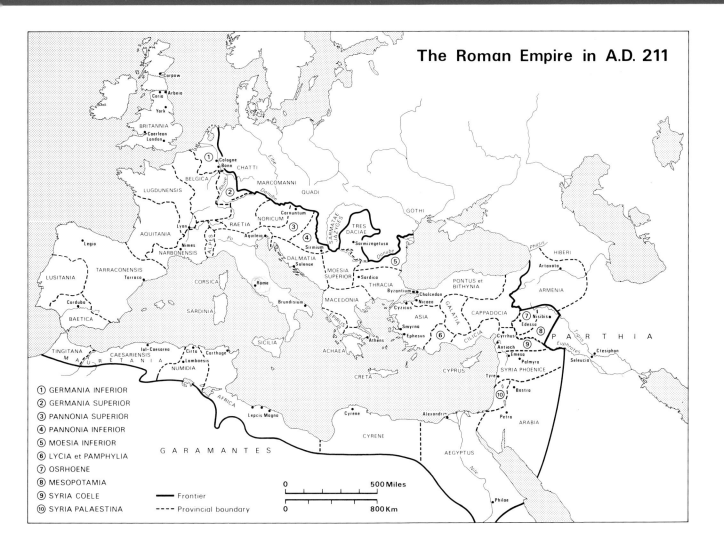

**The Roman Empire in A.D. 211**

① GERMANIA INFERIOR
② GERMANIA SUPERIOR
③ PANNONIA SUPERIOR
④ PANNONIA INFERIOR
⑤ MOESIA INFERIOR
⑥ LYCIA et PAMPHYLIA
⑦ OSRHOENE
⑧ MESOPOTAMIA
⑨ SYRIA COELE
⑩ SYRIA PALAESTINA

―― Frontier
----- Provincial boundary

0                    500 Miles
0                    800 Km

# GLOSSARY

**Amphitheatre**   an oval or circular arena for games or spectacles, surrounded by tiers of seats

**Aqueduct**   a channel for carrying water

**Aquilifer**   the standard bearer of the legion

**Auxiliaries**   the soldiers from the provinces allowed to fight in the Roman army

**Ballista**   a very large crossbow mounted on a cart

**Centurion**   man in charge of a century (a unit of 80–100 soldiers)

**Chariot**   a two-wheeled cart pulled by horses

**Citizen**   a freeman with certain privileges

**Cohort**   the tenth part of a legion

**Consuls**   the two men elected by the senate to hold supreme power for a year, during the republican period 509–49 BC

**Corn dole**   free distribution of grain

**Decimate**   to put to death one soldier in ten

**Dowry**   money or property brought by a girl or her family to her marriage

**Equites**   Roman middle class

**Forum**   open space in the middle of a town

**Gladiators**   men who fought either against each other or against animals at the games

**Greaves**   armour for the lower leg

**Insulae**   blocks of flats

**Latin**   language spoken by the Romans

**Legend**   a story handed down by tradition

**Legion**   largest division of the Roman Army, consisting of 4000–6000 men

**Legionaries**   members of a legion

**Numeri**   regiments of tribespeople from outside the Empire

**Praetorian Guard**   the emperor's bodyguard

**Republic**   a country without a king or queen, where the supreme power is held by someone who has been elected

**Senate**   the parliament of the Roman Empire

**Signifer**   the standard bearer of the century

**Stilus**   a sharp pointed instrument used for writing on wax (the other end was blunt, and used for smoothing over the wax, that is rubbing out)

**Taxation**   compulsory payment to the government

**Veteran**   an old soldier

**Vigiles**   Rome's fire brigade

# INFORMATION

## Money

The smallest coin was the bronze quadrans. Four of these made up the as, also a bronze coin, four asses made a sesterce, a silver coin, and four sesterces a denarius, another silver coin. The aureus was a gold coin. In the work sheet on the army, we are told that a cavalryman in Alexandria was paid in drachmas, Greek coins. Perhaps there was a shortage of Roman coins in Egypt and he had to be paid in whatever was available.

## Time

The Romans calculated the time by dividing the hours of daylight into twelve equal parts. The result was that an hour in summer for the Romans was approximately one hour and a quarter long, and in winter, three quarters of an hour. The twelve months of our year have the names given them by Caesar and Augustus. (Why is January called after the god Janus, who is said to have had two faces facing opposite ways?) They calculated the date by a rather complicated system of counting the days before or after three key days, the calends, the first day of the month, the nones, the fifth day in most months, but the seventh day in the 'long' months of March, May, July and October, and the ides, the thirteenth or the fifteenth day.

# FURTHER READING

## For younger readers

Burrell R.E.C. and Peter Connolly, *The Romans*, Oxford University Press.
Peter Connelly, *The Roman Fort*, Oxford University Press.
M. Corbishley, *The Ancient World*, Hamlyn.
Anita Ganeri, *Focus on Romans*, Watts.
Rupert Mathews, *Roman Soldiers*, Wayland.
Jon Nicol, *The Greek and Roman World*, Blackwell.
Marjorie and C.B.H. Querrell, *Everyday Life in Roman Times*, Carousel.

## For older readers

John Clare, *Roman Empire*, (*I was There* Series), Bodley Head.
R.J. Cootes and L.E. Snellgrove, *The Ancient World*, Longman.
Anthony Marks and Graham Tingay, *The Romans*, Usborne Illustrated World History.
Peter Salway, *Roman Britain*, Oxford University Press.

## Places to visit

There are a lot of Roman sites in Europe, North Africa, Egypt and the Middle East. If you are on holiday abroad, try the local museum or tourist information office to find out what there is to see in the vicinity. In Britain, as well as smaller museums with Roman exhibits, the following sites and museums are especially worth a visit: Hadrian's Wall at Housesteads, Northumbria; York Museum; Verulamium Museum and Theatre, St Albans, Hertfordshire; Roman Lighthouse, Dover, Kent; Lullingstone Villa, Eynsford, Kent; Fishbourne Palace and Museum, Chichester, Sussex; Cirencester Museum and Chedworth Villa, Cirencester, Gloucestershire; Roman Baths, Bath, Avon; Caerleon Museum and Amphitheatre, Gwent. Best of all, though, are Rome, Pompeii and Herculaneum.

## Acknowledgements

The Author and Publishers would like to thank the following for their kind permission to reproduce illustrations: Ancient Art and Architecture Collection for pages 4, 6 (top and bottom), 8–9, 10, 12, 13, 16–17, 17, 23, 25, 27, 33 (top and bottom), 38; Michael Holford 40; Kunsthistorische Museum, Vienna page 14; Erich Lessing frontispiece, pages 11, 15, 18, 19, 20–21, 21, 22, 24, 29, 32, 34, 35, 36, 43; Scala 5, 28–9, 37, 41.

# INDEX

Page numbers in **bold type** refer to illustrations.